"I CAN'T BEGIN TO DESCRIBE A DAY
AS WONDERFUL AS THIS.
ONE MARVEL AFTER ANOTHER,
EACH LASTING LESS THAN FIVE MINUTES...."

Claude Monet

To nature:
May she never stop.
To children: May they always create.
—B.R.

To Tom,
a perfect model of compassion
and patience.
Forever grateful for you.
—M.G.

MORNINGS WITH *Monet*

BY BARB ROSENSTOCK

ILLUSTRATED BY MARY GRANDPRÉ

ALFRED A. KNOPF
NEW YORK

He wakes to shadows the color of steeped tea, swings his sturdy legs from bed, buttons his pants, shrugs up suspenders, stretches a shirt over his broad belly, laces thick feet into tough boots, and grabs a battered felt hat on the way downstairs.

This man, Claude Monet, is rich, famous around the world.

He's on his way to work. It's 3:30 in the morning.

With each step, he notices the darkness shift;
he hurries out the emerald door of his pink stucco
house, past a palette he's rooted in earth: poppies,
nasturtiums, hollyhocks.

The summer mist fades his garden to a million
violet-gray tones, matching his bushy beard.

He crosses the road, strides around the water lily pond, through a meadow, to a rowboat in the reeds at the river's edge.

A man from Giverny—a gardener's helper—waits there.
He loads packages, climbs aboard with a hushed *Bonjour*,
patient the way those who work with plants, children, and
artists learn to wait—for some things take time to grow.
    He helps Monet balance his heft and unties the rope.
They cast off.

Monet heads into the current
of this river, the Seine.

OVER. DIP. PULL.

The same river that divides Paris,
where he was born.

OVER. DIP. PULL.

The same river that flows to the north coast

OVER. DIP. PULL.
The same river always—pushing back the way he
pushed against school, the family business,
a stable life indoors. Bold. Ever-changing.
This river he will try to capture.

near Le Havre, where he grew up.

They reach a flat-bottomed punt, anchored midstream like a boulder. Monet clambers aboard and opens the boat cabin's twin doors.

His helper unwraps fourteen paintings—unfinished oils that take months to dry, paired face to face with wood bars between to keep them from smearing.

He slips each numbered canvas into slats built into the deck, puts them in order dark to light, *un, deux, trois, quatre . . .* a series of transparencies: water, air, and memory.

Years ago, a reporter asked to see the great artist's studio.
Monet flung his arms toward the Seine. "That's my studio!"
But this *boat* is his studio.

Monet takes an easel folded against the cabin wall, turns a few
screws, sets it on the bow. He chooses ultramarine blue, cobalt
violet, cadmium yellow, lead white. He stirs in linseed oil,
grabs a rag, and selects his brushes.

It's the second summer he's worked here, and this is
his second studio boat.

Monet bought his first boat in Argenteuil—
when his first love still lived, and a loaf of bread
was a treasure.

He led a band of rebel artists then: Renoir, Degas,
Pissarro, Sisley, Morisot.

Rejected for using bright colors, tangled
brushstrokes; condemned for their impressions.

Now art dealers and collectors wait to see as Monet sees.
Monet waits only for the light.

A few rays break through; wet leaves droop over winding water.

He studies the river's hues, pulls the painting that matches this morning's mist up to the easel, brush in his right hand, palette loaded with paint in his left.

The studio boat rocks, but does not move from its spot. Only his eyes and hands move, and, of course, Nature herself. His challenge and his joy.

"*La nature ne s'arrête pas.*" Nature does not stop.

He picks up a dollop of deep purple on his brush.
Swooping and spreading shadows from palette to canvas.
Shaping without lines, seeing in patches of color.
Cream linen under bright green under dusty blue with
soft lavender smoothed on top.

Painting the river's colors, and the air around the colors.
Monet wipes his brow; it is not easy to paint air.

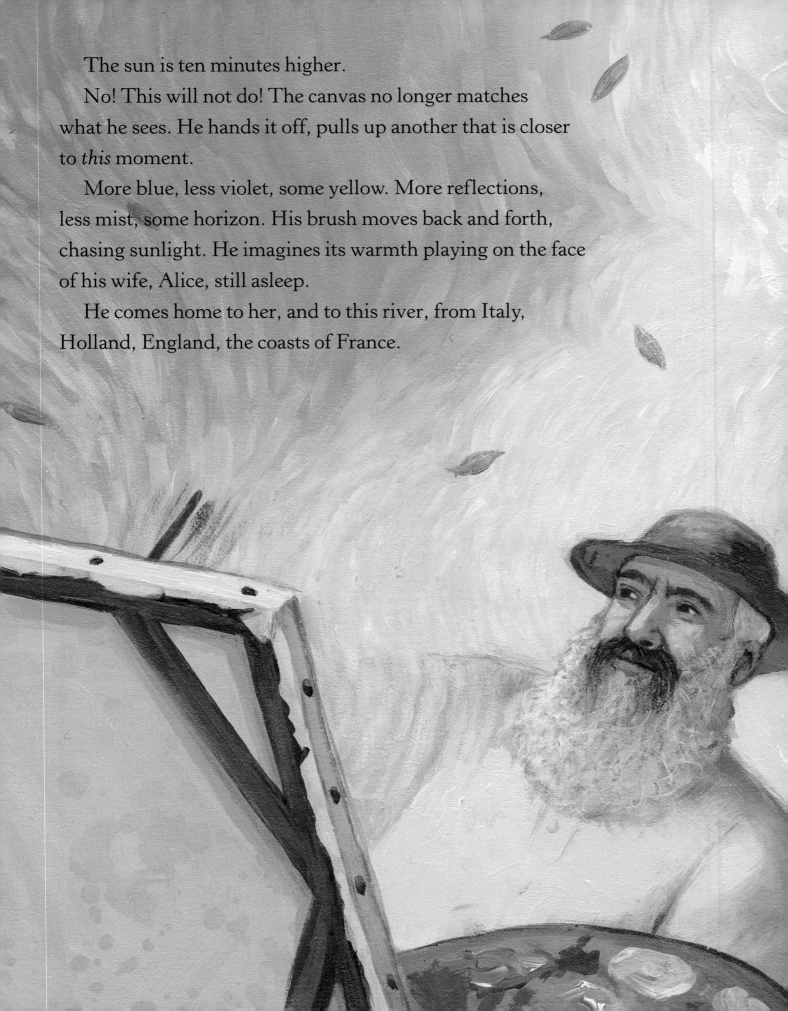

The sun is ten minutes higher.

No! This will not do! The canvas no longer matches what he sees. He hands it off, pulls up another that is closer to *this* moment.

More blue, less violet, some yellow. More reflections, less mist, some horizon. His brush moves back and forth, chasing sunlight. He imagines its warmth playing on the face of his wife, Alice, still asleep.

He comes home to her, and to this river, from Italy, Holland, England, the coasts of France.

For the right view, he's climbed wind-beaten cliffs, tumbled into ocean waves.

Painted blazing beaches while sun beat through his umbrella, and shady snowbanks while icicles hung from his beard.

Today, he unrolls the boat's awning to keep the hot sun from pushing him off the river too soon.

Fifteen minutes later, another canvas. Eleven minutes, and he shuffles again.

One lasts only six minutes on the easel.

FLICK.
DAB.
CURL.

Oils mix on the surface. In spots, he rubs with the rag.

His brush stutters a broken line of gauzy white
where land meets sky.
　　For three minutes, the water turns to glass.
Catch this river! Catch it!
　　He can only try. Artists try.

"I'd like to keep anyone from knowing how it's done," Monet has said.

But Alice knows; his children, dealers, friends, the cook
and gardeners all know.
Anyone who creates understands—that art is not magic.
It is work,
    and work,
        and work, and then . . .

IT IS MAGIC.

And today's morning magic is gone. The sun glares; none of his paintings match the scene. He scrapes the palette, stores brushes, caps tubes while his helper rewraps canvases. They close up and row back; Monet will need only a few more mornings on the Seine.

He steps onto the bank, walks through the meadow, around the pond. Soon he'll paint those water lilies . . .

but first, breakfast.

AUTHOR'S NOTE

Claude Monet lived near the Seine River his entire life and painted it more than any other subject. He was born in Paris, less than a mile from its banks, on November 14, 1840. When Monet was five, his father moved the family to the port city of Le Havre. Monet disliked school, but learned to draw there and, instead of working in the family ship supply business, wanted only to be an artist.

In Paris, he met other art students, among them Pissarro, Renoir, Sisley, Degas, and Morisot. Their work used visible brushstrokes, textures, and bright colors to paint modern subjects. Often rejected by the official "Salon" exhibition in Paris, they held the first independent art exhibition in spring of 1874. Many critics scorned Monet and his friends, calling them "lunatics" and their work "unfinished wallpaper." Taken from a Monet painting titled *Impression, Sunrise,* the group was sarcastically labeled "Impressionists." Now the most popular fine art style in the world, originally Impressionism was either disliked or ignored.

Monet struggled to support himself and his family for decades, until Impressionism became popular with collectors in the United States. By the 1890s, the now-wealthy Monet lived in a fine house along the Seine near Giverny. He began his "series" work—repeatedly painting the same subject (haystacks, poplars, a cathedral) in different light, weather, and times of day.

Monet's work on this book's subject, the *Mornings on the Seine* series, did not go smoothly at first. In fall of 1896, it rained for forty-one days. He finished only a few canvases from *le bateau atelier* (the studio boat) and waited out the winter. Most of the *Mornings on the Seine* canvases were finished in the summer of 1897.

Mornings on the Seine differs from Monet's earlier work—the paint surface is smoother and the colors more harmonized. Most of these canvases are square and had to be custom-ordered. Some are almost abstract— it is hard to tell up from down, or the real scene from its reflection. In June 1898, fifteen of the *Mornings on the Seine* series were exhibited in Paris. Critics praised Monet's ethereal scenes, and the exhibit dates were extended to accommodate the enthusiastic crowds.

Monet continued working on themes of water, air, light, and reflection. He spent the last thirty years of his life painting his iconic water lily pond in a number of series, the first begun in 1897. Monet originally created the pond by diverting a tributary of the Seine River near Giverny. In a very real way, in order to keep painting his beloved Seine as he aged, he brought the river home.

Caption information from left to right:

Branch of the Seine near Giverny © 2021 Art Resource Inc., New York. Photo credit: RMN-Grand Palais / Art Resource, NY

Morning on the Seine near Giverny © 2021 Art Resource Inc., New York. Photo credit: Art Resource, NY

Branch of the Seine near Giverny (Mist), 1897. The Art Institute of Chicago. Mr. and Mrs. Martin A. Ryerson Collection, 1933. 1156

The Studio Boat (Le Bateau-atelier), 1876. The Barnes Foundation

Water Lilies, 1906. The Art Institute of Chicago. Mr. and Mrs. Martin A. Ryerson Collection, 1933. 1157

SOURCES

Art Institute of Chicago. "Monet Paintings and Drawings at the Art Institute of Chicago," *Branch of the Seine near Giverny (Mist)*. publications.artic.edu/monet/reader/paintingsanddrawings/section/135612/135612_anchor

Fitzgerald, Desmond. "Claude Monet: Master of Impressionism," *Brush and Pencil*, 15(3), March 1905, pp. 181–195.

Gervais, David. "Unified Landscapes: Monet's Series Paintings," *Cambridge Quarterly*, 1991, 20(3), pp. 210–222.

House, John. *Monet: Nature into Art.* New Haven: Yale University Press, 1986.

La réplique du bateau-atelier de Claude Monet, video, youtube.com/watch?v=pNHGAlCkM7o

Millard, Charles W. "The Later Monet," *Hudson Review,* 31(4), Winter 1979, pp. 637–643.

Paul, Tanya, Helga Kessler Aurisch, Michael Clarke, and Richard R. Brettell. *Monet and the Seine: Impressions of a River.* Houston: Museum of Fine Arts, 2014.

Rewald, John. *The History of Impressionism.* New York: Museum of Modern Art, 4th ed., 1973.

Seiberling, Grace. *Monet's Series.* New York: Garland Publishing, 1981.

Skeggs, Douglas. *River of Light: Monet's Impressions of the Seine.* New York: Alfred A. Knopf, 1987.

Stuckey, Charles F., ed. *Monet: A Retrospective.* New York: Hugh Lauter Levin Associates, 1985.

Tucker, Paul Hayes. *Claude Monet: Life and Art.* New Haven: Yale University Press, 1995.

Tucker, Paul Hayes. *Monet in the '90s.* Boston: Museum of Fine Arts, 1989.

Wildenstein, Daniel. *Monet: Or the Triumph of Impressionism* (4 vols.). Berlin: Taschen, 1996.

ACKNOWLEDGMENTS

Thank you to Genevieve Westerby, Alyse Muller, Drew Erin Becker Lash, and Kathryn Kremnitzer, current and former Research Associates in the Department of European Painting and Sculpture at The Art Institute of Chicago, for their assistance with and review of the text and art.

THIS IS A BORZOI BOOK PUBLISHED BY ALFRED A. KNOPF

Text copyright © 2021 by Barb Rosenstock
Jacket art and interior illustrations copyright © 2021 by Mary GrandPré
All rights reserved. Published in the United States by Alfred A. Knopf,
an imprint of Random House Children's Books, a division of Penguin Random House LLC, New York.
Visit us on the Web! rhcbooks.com
Educators and librarians, for a variety of teaching tools, visit us at RHTeachersLibrarians.com
Library of Congress Cataloging-in-Publication Data is available upon request.
ISBN 978-0-525-70817-9 (hc) — ISBN 978-0-525-70818-6 (lib. bdg.) — ISBN 978-0-525-70819-3 (ebook)

The text of this book is set in 16-point Horley Old Style • The illustrations were created with acrylic paint and ink on illustration board.
Book design by Isabel Warren-Lynch and Sarah Hokanson

MANUFACTURED IN CHINA March 2021 10 9 8 7 6 5 4   First Edition
Random House Children's Books supports the First Amendment and celebrates the right to read.

"WHEN I WORK, I FORGET ALL THE REST."

Claude Monet